MW00944583

MY HEAVENLY FATHER NEVER FORSAKEN ME

SEIMEAKA SPOT CARTER

outskirtspress

DENVER, COLORADO

Outskirts Press, Inc.
http://www.outskirtspress.com

ISBN: 978-1-4787-7562-1

Outskirts Press and the "OP" logo are trademarks belonging to Outskirts Press, Inc.

PRINTED IN THE UNITED STATES OF AMERICA

Table of Contents

My Heavenly Father Never forsaken me.....

In today world there's so many different religions. There's so many religions but only one God. My story tell others how I accomplish and build a relationship with our heavenly father at the age fourteen. No matter what life brings your way. Having a relationship with God shall bring you through life. Hope my story will be a blessing to all.

Dear Readers,

Names, dates, places, and incidents in this book have been changed or omitted for a variety of reasons, including but not limited to the security, safety, and wellbeing of the people, places or agencies involved. Any resemblance to anyone living or dead is purely coincidental. I will leave it up to you the reader to realize what is what, who is who, and where is where. With this in mind this book is listed as work of fictionalized biography.

Seimeaka Spot Carter

THANKS TO MY HEAVENLY FATHER FOR HIS LOVE, GRACE, MERCY….

TO MY HUSBAND,ERNEST JR CARTER I LOVE YOU SO MUCH. THANKS FOR BEING SUCH A GREAT HUSBAND. THANKS SO MUCH FOR NOT GIVING UP ON ME. LOVE YOU !

TO MY BEAUTIFUL GIRLS SERENITY AND TAMMYEL, THANKS SO MUCH FOR ALL THE LITTLE WORDS OF ENCOURAGE-MENT. I LOVE YOU GIRLS …ALWAYS OUR LITTLE ANGELS

TO MY GRANDFATHER, CONTINUE TO REST IN PARADISE.. THANKS FOR ALL THE WISDOM AND KNOWLEDGE. WHICH IS A MUST, IN TODAY WORLD. LOVE ALWAYS

1

Vision of the Father

When I was a young girl. I wondered how my life would be as an adult. I could remember daydreaming about having my own family. A husband and kids, a home of our own. When you have seen so much in your childhood from adults. You want better for yourself as a adult. As a child I always felt stress, full of angry. I had no choice but to think positive, hope for the best in my adult-hood. What can I say about my childhood. I really didn't enjoyed being a kid. There wasn't really no fun times that I could remember. What I do remember in my childhood was the violence. Waking up some nights from the noise of my dad beating my mom. Which build so much anger inside of me. I don't remember my parents telling me they love me. I don't remember having family time together. I felt like I wasn't love. Yes I do remember having a roof over my head, food on the table and cable, etc.

A childhood is not only about providing for a child. A childhood is also about spending time with a child. Showing that child you love them. You gain a bond with a child when time is put in. No moments of laughter, no moments of love. As a child I grew up in a small town called Thibodaux. Thibodaux is located in Louisiana. I was born and raised in Thibodaux. In the household was my mom, older brother and two little sisters. My mom was a single mom. My dad was in and out our lives. Our grandfather played a great role of a father to us. My grandfather was a very wise man. He was a man full of wisdom, knowledge, love. He enjoyed sharing his wisdom, knowledge, love. Today I'm so grateful for him playing a role in my childhood. The memories of the abuse in the household, with my parents, my grandfather love over power it all. Some would say I'm humble always stayed quiet. I kept a lot inside. Like I stated before I would always daydream and vision better. I remember always saying "When I get older this pattern that's going on will not happen in my household. I will not allow my husband and kids to not know how much I love them. I promise to show them I love them. Everyone have a story to tell. Some rather keep their story inside. Some rather share. When it's a story about the heavenly father, you must share it. You can't keep stories with him hidden inside. When I was a young girl my grandfather would share stories about the heavenly father. Our grandparents would bring us to church on Sunday. I use to hear the preacher speak on the heavenly father. I wanted to know him more. I wanted to know the one that's so powerful, the one, no one have seen. I heard how he can move mountains. He created me and every living thing. I knew one day, I would seek this powerful name. I wanted to see the great results. My grandfather would tell me, call on his name when you're going through problems, and everything shall be alright! Being a child, in a child mind. I thought how can everything be alright. I called on him, my parents still having violence in the household. I called on him and I'm still making bad grades. I called on him still angry everyday. Now since I'm a adult, It's more than just a call. You must accomplish a relationship with the heavenly father. I realized my grandfather had a relationship with the father. A relationship when he spoke on behalf of the father, tears would roll down his eyes. Then right then and there I knew the heavenly father was serious. Even though I felt like my childhood didn't hold no good

---

memories. I knew the more and more I called on the heavenly father, I will be able to conquer anything. I continue to daydream and vision. Each time I vision, I drew my visions. Each time I daydream, I've daydream with my heavenly father in the picture. Each time I would picture him in my pictures. My pictures was beautiful and full of glow. My visions always appeared with a big light. My visions always felt so real. Each vision that he gave me always came true..

SEIMEAKA QUOTE

Move forward and leave your past behind,

Vision positive, Draw your vision,

Put God in your vision, walk into your vision..

2

Love from the Heavenly Father

I once read that when your mother and father forsake you God will never. Those words was written for a reason. Yes we live in a world where, the kids are disobedience. Yes we live in a world where, the parents don't know how to love their kids. You have kids that's violence against their parents and you have parents that's violence against their kids. I realized most the time for a child to be violence against their parents they're looking for attention. They want their parent to acknowledge something is wrong with them. The parents should show them they care by getting them the help they need. Most of the time parents that hurts their children, have suffer past hurt themselves. They never got the help they needed as a child. They find themselves growing up, being adults, hurting others. They end up pasting all that hurt down to their own children. When the children have no understanding of why they're going through so much with their parents. Their parents have been hurt so badly. They kept so much inside. Then they expect their kids to be perfect. When they never had a perfect life themselves. They can't show love because they never been loved. Some learn to stop the way they was raise, others let the pattern linger. I remember when I was a preteen. I was looking for love. I wanted someone to show me. I wanted someone to tell me. I wanted to just know that I value to someone. I knew my grandfather told me about the heavenly father. I was changing, growing and wanted to see what the world had to offer. I wanted to explore. I wanted to go out and see for myself. Now since I'm older, I know my heavenly father said go my child and see for yourself. Trust you'll come to me. When I felt forsaken by my parents, I was searching for love in the world. I felt like there was no way the world, would forsake me. I wanted love and I went out searching for it. Searching for it, not knowing that I can really get hurt. I was young and wonder how worst can things get. My parents showed they didn't care, so guess I didn't care. Yes, what a mind of a lost child. At age twelve I started dating. I started having feeling for boys. My mind was focus on boys, more than my school work. I found myself sneaking out the house. Thinking back I realize I could of got killed, anything could of happen. When I was gone at night. I always wonder what would happen if I was to get caught. I never got caught sneaking out the house. I found myself getting drunk. I found myself smoking. I just wanted attention. I needed to think different, I needed to feel different. Once I realized my momma wasn't checking up on me at night. I knew right then an there she could of care less. Today I'm a mother of two beautiful girls, I make sure I check on them every night. I tell them every night,,, I love them, before they close their eyes. I never want my girls to feel like I'm not giving them the time. Never want them to feel like I'm not a concern mother. I walk in their rooms at night to check on them. They always say, "momma " that's you? I response, "yes," my loves, I'm just checking on you guys. Now they know they'll never be able to play that role I played in my younger days.

When you're a child, you act like a child, but when you become an adult you leave your childish behavior behind. As much as I was looking for love. I had love inside of me. I also was loved by the heavenly father. As much as I wanted to my mother love. I loved her deeply. When I was a young girl I would pray for her protection. The mother and daughter relationship wasn't there. We really disconnected, when she caught me about to have sexton with a young guy. I felt shame because I got caught of course. I also felted like,, wow you care? The one who down me. The one who gave birth to me but made me felt so ugly inside. I thought maybe this may be a way that she'll get rig of me. No because I was the one that need to wash dishes, fold clothes, mind my little sisters. Hell, I was a child!! I wanted to do things a child did. When you're pulled away from those things. You tent to do other things. I wanted to be involved in cheerleading, dancing, much more. No instead I was at home cleaning. I thank God I learned those things while I was young. Now I'm a adult, think I'm hypnotize. I find myself can't stop cleaning. I also think someone going to fuss me for not cleaning my own house. Don't get me wrong if there was anything I've learned from my mom. It was to keep a clean house. My God, I think I over does it sometimes. I want my kids to enjoy being a kid. I want them to have good memories. I promise them they should enjoy their childhood. I thank God I was able to change things for my girls. I also thank God I was able to learn from my pass experience. I am to share with my girls, my bad decisions. Where they wouldn't go down the wrong path. We go through things in life for a reason. To benefit ourselves and others. That happening in my younger day with that guy. Looking back I hope I didn't think that was love. Love is much more then having intercourse. My parents knew they was involved at a young age. Instead of condemning me. Explain to me the out comes of having intercourse at a young age. I believed when you make mistakes while you're young. You should at least give your kids advice. As parents we should talk our kids before they go out and do the same. My parents had every right to be upset. Should you're upset by punishment not downing the child. Putting a child down, only push them back towards the wrong road. When I felt so down and lost. I called on my heavenly father. I learned to lift myself up, when no one would. I'm smart, I'm beautiful. I can do all things. Those was the words I'll tell myself. To keep myself from feeling down. Parents should never give their children negative words, to put them down. It stayed in my mind and heart, that my parents showed me signs of not caring. I remember when I got my first job at Burger king. I was so excited. I couldn't wait to get all the things I needed. My school needs, my personal needs, much more. I also was saving. I always would say, soon I'm going to save enough money to move out. I knew I was to young to move out. Truly, I couldn't wait until I was old enough to move. I needed to be happy. I needed to be in an environment, where there was happiness. On Sunday's everyone went to church. Return from church seems like every word that was taught at church went through one ear out the other. Words of love was never really shown in our house. I stated house because it never felt like a home. Home is where the love begins. Home is a place you'll never want to leave. I can't speak for my siblings but as for me I was miserable. I was a teen, I was always depress. I ended up moving in with my dad, for about a couple of months. My reason for moving in with my dad. My mom and I had a argument over my first paycheck. I was so excited to cash my first check. She already plan out my check for me. She seen an item at Big Lots she wanted. I felted like since I was buying my personal items etc. Why? Why is a piece of furniture so important, to you? On the way to cash my check. Me and my mom argue. I walked into the store to cash my check. On the way coming out. The car said, "Look for me," I walked back into the store with tears rolling down my eyes. I called my best friend Kasey Tubbs. Kasey and I became good friends in junior high. When I was down she was there to help me. She came and pick me up. Eyes filled with tears. I couldn't believe my mother would rather choose to put herself before me. Today, I'm afraid to put myself before my kids. I work hard to make sure they have. I want my kids to know their more important than my needs and wants. Evidently my needs or wants was not important to my mom or dad. My dad and mom was appearing to be the same. Living with my dad was even horrible. My dad showed me to my face that he didn't care. He wanted me out his way. His home was for him, his wife and his daughter. My time at my dad house had expired. I knew going back to my mom house was going to expired also. It was so sad to know I was young with no place that felt like home. Who wants to run away from home, where your love ones are. I remember praying and praying to God to cover me. I continue to stay humble,and allow God to move. I keep reminding myself God had a plan. Seem like all I was going through, God was enlightening me on life. I just came out a bad situation and had to be mindful of what I involve myself in. I met a new guy. I really was attractive to him. I prayed to God about him. For some reason I seen more in me and him. I prayed to God, that one day we will get married and complete a family. I knew I shouldn't have been thinking about marriage at fifteen. Our relationship was getting closer. He such a gentlemen. He listened to all my problems. He also understood all my problems. I told him I was saving up for transportation. I was walking back and forth to work and I wanted better for myself. He promise he'll help me get the car. He kept his words. I was so excited about my first car. God reveal to me he was the one. He was the one because he cared. God showed me that one day we would get marry and have a family. It all sounded like a fairytale. Deep down inside I knew it was real. As much as the thoughts of my parents appear in back of my mind. I was finally feeling loved.

SEIMEAKA QUOTE

When the people who suppose to love you show you they don't love you. Know that God loves endures forever.

3

God Got A Plan

We can write our dreams, we can write our plans. The best plans is God. His plans always work out the best. When he plans, it always come out with great results. He never promise us that the road would be easy. If we fall, he'll pick us up. We must keep our eyes and mind on him. It took a accident to get me to my path. I was on my way to visit my guy friend, before I left to go visit him. My mom and I had a argument. I still decided to make my way to visit him. That day I thought, I was going to lose my life. My guy friend and I, his sister and a good friend war traveling to the store. We was driving down the bridge. Soon as we drove down the bridge. The car begin to flip. I remember holding on to the seat really tight. I remember the windshield crashing. My face and head was full of glass. I remember praying to God. God please, please protect us. God showed up! Everyone was rush to hear hospital. People on the roadway couldn't believe we were still alive. I believe in miracles. We are living testimonies and miracles. All four of us was hospitalized. All the others family was there ,at the hospital. My family, my family no where to be found. It was time for me to be released out the hospital. Since I was a minor, I needed my parents there to sign the release papers. My mom was contacted and inform of what happen. Her response to the doctor was, I'm at work and I'm not leaving. We must forgive people but I can tell you this weekend will never forget.

Regardless of what goes on with parents and their child. A child is in need of their parents. No matter what the circumstances may be parents much play the role of parents. Even tough me and my father didn't have a relationship he came to sign the release papers. The papers was sign but I still didn't have a home to go to. In the car with my dad. My dad asked, "Where I'm dropping you off to? In my mind I didn't have a clue, where I was going. That moment I begin to pray to myself. Heavenly Father , I have no where to go. Heavenly Father guide me, shield me. Heavenly Father I need you! I was sixteen and it was time to go out in the world. My dad drop me off by my guy friend house. My guy friend lived with his grandmother. His parents passed away when he was a young boy. I didn't feel comfortable asking his grandmother if I can live with them. His grandmother must have thought, how can her parents not have no concern about their child. I don't know if my mom thought she was hurting me. Maybe she thought, Let her go out in the world. She'll come back crying. Hope she didn't wish bad come my way. God told me, "Seimeaka while you was in your mother womb. I created you, I shall protect you. I bless her with you. When a mother or father forsake their child God will never will. I was hurt knowing I had parents that felt that way about me. I also knew I had a great father. I can call on anytime and anyday. Remembering what my grandfather said, I knew all was going to be ok. I needed his love. The love that endures forever. My guy friend grandmother agree to me living there. I thank God for her. I thank God for placing it in her heart and mind to allow me to live there. I knew God had a plan. A plan for us both! If I just trust and believe in him, it all will work out fine. I live with his family for about four months. He promised me that we was going to get our own place. There was times I cried and felt so hurted. He promised we'll get through all this. With his help and God first. I believe I was going to get through, all I was facing. Soon we was moving into our first apartment. Lord knows I didn't have a clue about living on my own. I was only sixteen. Sixteen and living in my own apartment. It was different but I knew with God , we was going to get through. I never was taught about living on my own. Never was taught the responsibility to living on my own. My heavenly father gave me all the knowledge of those things. All I needed help with, I asked and he gave it to me. There was still a whole lot of learning for me. One thing I realized, looking back. I didn't know how to truly love. I knew he was going to help me with that situation. Coming out the situation with my parents. I didn't really trust anyone. Having negative feelings about both parents. I felt like I was on my own. I had to learn to really defend myself. Living with my guy friend. It was very hard to get adjusted to. No matter what I was feeling. I stayed prayed up! Through all my tears and pain. I managed to always stay prayed up. Time was pasting, still manage staying on my own. I wanted to attend school. My mom had drop me out of school. My guy friend grandmother encourage me to get my learning. As much as I wanted to go back to school. There was no way of her signing me back in school. I believed my mom wanted me to accept not getting an education. Deep down inside I wanted better. I couldn't give up on getting my high school diploma. I had to prove to my parents. I'm better than what they thought of me. I mat be they child , here on earth, but I'm a child of the most high power king. My heavenly father teaching me and guiding me is the best learning ever. Not only did I had to learn but my guy friend also. We both was in a process of learning. My guy friend and me learning together was wonderful. It was really hard for me to trust a man. Especially when you came from a violence household. Seeing my dad fight my mom. I thought it was okay to fight. I would look for my guy friend to hit me. Just so I can fight back harder. He use to tell me,

Girl I don't want to fight you. I remember him telling me. Are you cray? A man should never hit a woman. W was very young. He wanted to have fun. He wanted to go out with his friends. I just edit wanted him with me all the times. I found myself trying to watch every move he made. I just didn't have it in me to trust anyone. I realized I couldn't change a man. I didn't make him.

SEIMEAKA QUOTE

In life we want people to be the way, we want them to be. Maybe there's some things within ourselves, we need to change. Be willing to change yourself. Don't focus on trying to change others.

4

Bundle of Joy

I had no choice but to learn how to change. I was seventeen when I found out, I was pregnant with my first daughter. I was bringing a child into the world. How awful would it be to still have nasty ways. I sure didn't want my daughter to be raise in a unstable environment. I needed to change so I could teach her how to love, care, and respect others. My guy friend and I was new to parenting. Not having a relationship with my own parents. I had a lot of learning about parenting. I prayed to my heavenly father for help. Heavenly father teach me how to be a great mother. Heavenly father teach us how to be great parents. Heavenly father teach us how to love, so we can love our child. God is love. He love when his children is willing to love. We couldn't wait until our baby girl arrived. We couldn't wait to love her. Knowing we had a little one on the way, was bringing us together. Preparing for her was such a blessing. I promised to love her. I promised to protect her. I promised to teach her about the heavenly father. My daughter is my parents first grandchild. I thought to myself, my daughter, coming into this world. Would have gave them a second chance. Give her the love you never gave me. All I been through with my parents. I still allowed them in our lives. One thing about being a child of the most high he will not allow you to hold anything in your heart. You have to learn how to forgive. Forgive so you can be able to move on. Forgive others for yourself. Forgiveness is for you, not for them. My earthly parents and I was gradually pulling together. I realized all that happen in the past. Most stay in the past. I was bringing a bundle of joy into the world. I had no choice but to let go. I was so grateful for my mom, blessing us with a baby shower. For a while, I believed that she have changed. I can't judge people. I can state my opinions.

I realized some people will do good for you. Then they'll turn around and hurt you. I rather someone to keep the gifts and money. Just show me genuine love. I want someone to show the love me by showing they care. Caring for someone showing concern. We was young parents and we really loved our unborn child. I care for her by making sure I ate right. I care by making sure I took care of myself while I was pregnant. Young parents and we was learning a lot. We was founding out who was for us and who wasn't. There was talk of me being a young mother pregnant. Yes I was young. I was living on my own. With the help of my heavenly father we had our own apartment. Own transportation, working hard to take care of our responsibilities. The lies, the stories, I couldn't let it get to me. Once again I couldn't let it get to me. I needed to be strong for our daughter. The night before our little girl arrived. My guy friend had propose to me. So much coming all at once.

With tears of joy. She was here. Such a beautiful, gorgeous , wonderful blessing. Our little girl, such a beauty. We named her Serenity Da' Zariah Carter. Her name came from the Serenity Prayer. God give me the wisdom and understanding to accept the things I can not change. I had to learn, all I had been through. I couldn't change. I had no choice but to let go and let God. Soon after I had Serenity. I couldn't wait to go home and cuddle with her. It was my time as a parent to show my own child how

I can love her. Enjoy every moment with her. My fiancé felt the same way. We was young parents but with the help of our heavenly father, we was doing great. Serenity was growing very fast. My parents was involved with Serenity. Serenity enjoyed my two little sisters. They adore every moment with her. My dad came around few times. Living on my own, I really didn't focus on them. My main concern was God, and having a loving stable family. The more and more importantly got closer to God. The more and more I got closer to God. I was able to find out who was for me, Who was against me. I realize with God over me. There was no weapon that could format against me. I made sure, I taught our baby girl about the heavenly father. I also made sure she knew how to pray to him. The bibles states teach a child, while they're young. When they get older, they shall not depart from what you taught them. Later on in life. All I have steer in my daughter will shows. I will sit back and say well done. I promised to change the pattern. Give my daughter all the love, care, support. For a while, I was a stay at home mom. I enjoyed all the crying moments. Getting up at night. I enjoyed reading to her and of course spoiling her. My fiancé went back to work. The days without him, we truly missed him. A new baby, we found out how expensive things were. Baby bills, food etc. Through it all we was living. Living but it was time for me, to find a job. My fiance job was slow. I really needed to help. I realized he couldn't do it all alone. I hated being away from Serenity but it was time for mommy to go to work. I needed to do what was best for our family. Being a mother, I realized there's times you have to let go. Let go, when they go to school, college, much more. When I got a job, Serenity was off to daycare. I cried when I drop her off. She cried when I left her. I had to learn to trust people. In my mind is just kept wondering, if someone would hurt my daughter. The feeling from my family. I had to gain my trust for others. When I was away from Serenity. I prayed who ever care she was in they'll protect her. In this world we have to learn to trust others. It's hard but we have to put trust in others. I knew she was ok. She was protected by the heavenly father. I realized our children are only lent to us. We never know just how long were able to keep them. We must always give them kisses, cuddle them, praise them, hold them tightly. Most of all love them!!. She was growing so fast. Time really goes by fast. Every moment must be cherish!

SEIMEAKA QUOTE

We must teach our children about the heavenly father. We are not promise to them and they're not promise to us. Our heavenly father is promise to us. He shall never leave us nor forsake us.......

5

Better As One

We have been girlfriend and boyfriend for a little too long. We also have been engaged for a while. It was time to become one. In 2005, we tied the knot. Serenity was a toddler. We was getting older. God was leading us in the right direction. His directions and orders are always better. We became one and God had a wonderful blessings right after. My relationship with my heavenly father brings so much happiness and joy. I 'my able to hear from him. The more and more importantly seek him. The more and more he showed up. The same year God had spoke to me. He told me he was going to bless my family with our own home. I was nineteen. I was working as a waitress. My husband was twenty-two. He was working as a welder helper. We talked about moving. We didn't have a clue, it was going to be so soon.

When God tell you something, you must stop and listen. You must obey. He'll never tell you any wrong. He shall never forsake you. One day, I was on my way to work. God spoke to me. Every morning, after dropping Serenity off to daycare. It was my time with my heavenly father. Time to pray and praise him, conversation with him. That day my heavenly father said," Go straight to the bank." When you get to the bank, tell the you're there to apply for a home loan. Deep in my mind I knew with

God all things are possible. To be honest, I did had a little doubt in my mind. I was like, I'm only nineteen. I have no credit. I don't know anything about owning my own home. How is this possible, once again with God all is possible. Regardless of the thoughts. I walked in the bank with faith. Faith of a mustard seed. Entering into the bank. I was asked," Are you here for a checking account? Do you like to open a saving account? My response was no I'm here for a home loan. To be honest I was nineteen but looked fourteen. The loan specialist asked," Are you old enough for a mortgage loan? Yes I am. Her face looked puzzle. She said, Do you know what you're asking for? Yes I do. She then begin to tell me what all the requirements for a home loan. I went along and said yes I do. In the back of my mind I was like,now heavenly father. Did you hear the lady? I have to get approve. I was already approved. My heavenly father was my cosigner. He wouldn't of sent me there to fail me. I gave the loan specialist all the information she needed. She responded, " I will get back with you," " to let you know if you're approve." I left the bank. I got into the car. I remember saying," okay father thank you!" He's response was get ready to pack. I told my husband about how I obeyed my heavenly father. I wanted my husband to be with me but I needed to go along. He didn't believe. His faith wasn't strong. God still needed to build him up. His response, when I told him, was girl are you crazy? Do you know all you have to do, for a home loan? I said, yes I know now. In his mind, he was like, I don't believe it. He didn't believe we was moving. Few days went by. I still haven't heard from the loan specialist. No words, but I still believed my heavenly father. I packed up. I even went out and brought new items for our home. I knew time was at the essence. I remember this day like it was yesterday. I was off from work. The phone rung. I looked at the caller ID. It was the baking calling. I answered, Hello this is Seimeaka speaking. The voice on the other end, responded, Hello Seimeaka. This is the loan specialist, I'm calling to give you information about the home loan. Her response was,you did get approved. I was stuck!! Seimeaka Seimeaka start looking for a home. I was still stuck. I froze for seconds. Then I unfroze myself. I started crying and praise God! Heavenly father, Heavenly father thank you. We was moving into our first home. When my husband came home. He could tell something was different. Serenity and I was having a Lil party. Ok, Seimeaka what's going on? We got approved!!! All we need to do is look for a home. He still didn't believe. I guess it took the U-Haul and the signing of the home, for him to believe. Yes all of that for him to believe. I realized in life everyone is not build like you. We all have different minds. We all have different hearts. We all accept things differently. Some feel like so much is impossible. Some feel like so much is possible. The ones who believe all is possible, are the ones who knows God. Married to my husband. I realized he didn't realize how powerful God was. I loved him the same even tough he still didn't believed me. I had faith in God that one day he would believe and draw closer to God. We have been married for four months. The fifth month God bless us with our home. When you do the right things by God he will bless you. He knows our heart. He knew we came together in marriage for the right reasons. The right reasons was true love. I believe true love, honorable marriage brings blessings.

Seimeaka Quote

Marriage is honorable in all..

Hebrews 13:4

When you marry someone for the wrong reasons, it will never work out. When you marry someone for the right reasons, it shall work out.

6

Life, Trials

Life is like a roller coaster. There will be some ups and downs. Having a relationship with the heavenly father you will be able to get through those ups and downs. No matter what comes our way. We must know that our heavenly father shall take care of us. He'll be there to protect you along the way. Marriage, A new home, a new baby. My heavenly father does everything perfect. He bless us with a new home. He also knew a new bundle of joy was on the way. I was about two months in my pregnancy, moving into the new home. Everything was happening so fast. So much was coming towards my way. I had to keep faith. Our heavenly father would never put so much on us. He knows what we can handle. He knows what we can't handle. I realized when you have a divine relationship with the father. The enemy will find a way to get through. The enemy would use close people to hurt you. We have to remember. No weapon format against us shall prosper. No matter what came my way. I continue to stay prayed and connected to the heavenly father. Our heavenly father also want us to learn. What type of father would he be if he never let us see our wrongs. My husband and I had a lot of learning. In the new home and getting ready for our new baby. We was beginning to face hard times. There was times, when I felt like it was just so much. There was times I felt like giving up. Then I'll look at where God brought me from. I'll say," I must go on. I'll look at my family, my father bless me with. I say," I can't give up. He help me get this far, he'll never leave me nor forsake me. Every time I felt distance from the father. He always would show up. It was his way of showing me, he never left me. I was about six months pregnant. I was jotting down baby names. For some reason, I couldn't come to a decision with a name. He appeared to me. He said, "My child, this child will be another little girl. You should name her after her father mother. My husband lost his mother when he was a young boy. He stated a few times in our relationship he wish his mother was here. Naming our second daughter after his mother was God way of showing him. How real God is. I had to obey God, no matter what. No 3D ultrasound, God explained to me, our little girl will resemble her father mother. I knew once again my father was right. My husband mother name is Tammie. As much as I hated Tammie. I obeyed God and name her after her. When Tammyel came into this world, she resemble her grandmother. My husband grandmother seen Tammyel. She said, my my this is Tammie all over again. I looked back at pictures of my husband mother. Our daughter look so much like her. My husband begin to believe my relationship with God wasn't no joke. Everything I'll tell him always came to past. I wanted him to get close to our heavenly father. I wanted him to have that feeling. The feeling of knowing with God all is possible. I knew it wasn't my place to force him to believe. God always have a way of showing up to us. He have a way of proving who he is. Before a blink of an eye, God showed him. Our little girls was getting older. We enjoy being parents. I enjoyed the family moments. I can't go days without saying," I love you to my family." I made sure I changed the pattern of the way I grew up. As much as I loved having a family. Family problems was being faces. I realized no one have a perfect family. If anyone say they have a perfect family, they're lying. In a family, you're going to have some dis-agreements. The goal is to come together, talk the situations out. When arguing, never leave the same way. You may go in angry, but leave out happy. Learn how to make up and continue to love. Our girls was getting older. My husband and I had to change the way we disagree. The way your kids are, possibly the way the parents are. Kids pays attention to everything. There little minds absorb things, we think they don't know. As parents we have to be mindful, of what behavior we have around our kids. Hardship was steady coming towards my family. I was so stress. I tried my best to keep a smile on my face for my girls. I seen how much my girls loved me. I hated for them to see me upset. Me being upset only would make them upset. When I say, life is like a roller coaster, it is. You may go up and you make come down. No mat-ter how I much I felt down. I continue to look up. Our heavenly father never promise us our life would be perfect. If we keep our eyes on him, he shall keep us in perfect peace. In so many words, the enemy have a way of coming to destroy. When you have that connection with God. The enemy wouldn't stand a chance. He will try his best to destroy you. He will try his best, to get you to give up. Never give up! No matter what comes your way. You must keep pushing forward. We're going to fall but it's all about getting up. Never let the enemy win at his own game. We are children of the most high power. We always win!

SEIMEAK QUOTE

We are children of the most high power. Our heavenly father holds all the power. When you're down. Keep looking up!!!!

7

Child of the Most High

I'm a child of a king. Being a child of God doesn't mean you're not going to face problems. Our problems can be our test. A test to test our faith. A test to see if we're going to give up. I was being tested in so many ways. One test was we was close to losing our home. I was back at work, but I was only part-time. Ernest wasn't working. We was facing hardship trying to pay our mortgage. Once you get behind, it's hard to catch back up. If you're behind on your mortgage. Trust it will be hard for any loan companies, to approve you for any loans. Which makes plenty sense. Why would someone approve you for a loan? If you can't make payments on your current loan. Being the mother I am. Most important was making sure my family had food and electricity, love. We was steady falling behind. Soon, we were being serve foreclosure paperwork. Before we have received the paperwork. I asked family and friends for help. What I didn't stop to do is, think about who bless us with the home. My family and my friends didn't. God bless us with the home. I needed to called on him. My daughter Serenity who was three at the time came to me. She said," momma this is our home." God gave us this home"." We're not moving." Tears in my eyes, I grap Serenity and hug her and said," Yes baby yes." I got on my knees and cried out to God. I asked him to forgive ,for taking my eyes off him. Soon after I finish praying unto God. God gave me a name of a man who would help us. I looked up the man name. I contacted him and told him our situations. My husband and I met with the man. The same day we met him. The same day our home was save. Some may ask, " How can you tell others you was about to lose you home? In life we going to face problems. Everyone problems are different. Some shall share to help others. Don't be full of pride and hide situations. God have ways of teaching you. What he taught me was responsibilities. He want us to learn the right way so we can benefit ourselves. The feeling of almost about to lose our home was miserable. In my mind , I was thinking that we would have to start over. Put not having two stable jobs, wasn't going to help at all. Our heavenly father want us to lean on his understanding, not ours. From his understanding, we wasn't going anywhere. We sure didn't. We still in our home, thanks to my heavenly father. There was some family and friends who we called on laugh and talk negative. I realize you must leave people up to God. Don't treat people the way they treat you. I do know telling God all your problems is the best you can do. I was getting ready to give up. I kept the faith. I did what my heavenly father told me to do. In life problems will come back to back. It's up to you if you're willing to go back and forth. Being a child of God go for it. Remember, when God give you something you never have to worry about him taking it away. God made sure our home was save. My husband and I manage to get full times jobs. I was so afraid of facing hard times. I was working three jobs. Working three jobs, I was away from my family. I life we want the best for our families. Some decisions we make in life may not be the best our families. It not only affect you, but it affect the people who love you. How was it affecting the people I love? My kids was upset because I was to tired to spend time with them. My husband was bothered. I didn't want to give him time. My marriage was starting to crumble. Me working so hard, didn't give my husband the right to do what he have done. I didn't know what it had to take for him to understand. How powerful my relationship with God. My heavenly father reveal to me in a dream. My husband was going to commit adultery. The vision of the woman was shown in the dream. God also explain to me, my dream was going to come to pass. He told ,"when it comes to pass," Don't throw stone for stone. My heavenly father told me," My child I'm preparing you for what is about to happen." My heavenly father reminded me that ,I must obey him. He told me I know you're going to be upset. You must keep the faith. You must leave your husband up to me. Don't you try to fight the battle. To be honest with all who's reading this. I disobeyed him. I told my husband of what I dreamed. Of course he denied it. Once again my husband thought I was crazy. To be honest at that moment. When I found out what I dream was real. I became crazy. I wanted to hurt him the same way he hunted me. I wanted him to feel the way I felted. The enemy knew I was upset. There was so many men ,coming into my direction. For some reason I just couldn't get involved with another man. Knowing I was still married. Everything that my husband own in our household. I destroyed it. The pain of being lied too and cheating on. I wanted to destroy him. I had to keep in my mind. There two little girls looking up to me. I just couldn't believe all we have just been through. Why would he put me through all of this. We just came out a hardship, close to losing our home. This, Is what I deserved? To be honest, I didn't know how to forgive him. I really didn't want to forgive him. God appeared to me again. My child do you remember your vows? "For better or worst," "For rich or poor," For sickness or health," In marriage you're going to face some problems There going to be times. When you feel like giving upon each other. Times of disagreements. Times of sickness, to see if each other will stand by each other side. In marriage we must put God first. A healthy marriage is strong, when God is included. Marriage also is about coming together as one. Being hurt in my marriage. It brought up my pass hurt from my parents. He knew all the nights of tears and pain in felt from them. Why would he put me through this again? I realize we're going to be hurt by people. The ones you love the most can hurt you. People also can change. We have to learn to forgive. In marriage hard times will make one another strong. Forgiving my husband was for me. I needed to forgive, so I could move on and continue to be strong.

SEIMEAKA QUOTE

The good word states in Luke 6:37 Judge not and ye shall not be judged. Condemn not and ye shall not be condemned. Forgive an ye shall be forgiven...

8

Forgiveness

Forgiveness if for you. I had no choice but to forgive my husband. I needed to forgive him for myself. I woke up one morning. I couldn't see anything. I remember screaming to my husband, " I can't see!" His response was , "Your eyes are open." My eyes were open, but everything appeared dark. When I would move my eyes I would feel pain. The pain was in the back of my eyes. My husband rushed me to the hospital. I remembered him being there with me. I also remember, him asking me to forgive him. I needed to be heal. In the hospital, so many different test was taken. Doctors was trying to find the problem. A MRI detected tumors on my brain. What is MS? Multiple Sclerosis is a disease that damage at least two separate areas of the central nervous system (CNS),which includes the brain, spinal cord and optic nerves. In my case my brain and optic nerve was damaged. My optic nerve being damaged case me not to see. I stayed in the hospital for weeks. I received Natalizumab injections. The injections is giving to reduce the ability of inflammatory immune cells. Natalizumab prevents relapses and vision loss. I was diagnosed with this disease. In my mind I did not accept it. I forgave my husband in my heart. Once the heart can forgive. The mind can forget. Coming home, knowing what I just faced. I didn't stop to think of what we just been through in our marriage. I was slowly getting my vision back. I continue to pray and keep the faith. I kept saying to myself I walked by faith not by sight. I also remembered the song. Amazing Grace, How sweet the sound, I once was Blind, Now I can see! I kept encouraging myself. I also had my kids and husband encouraging me. My two little sisters also was a big help with their nieces. I thank God so much for their help. God also sent a young lady to come pray for me. I thank God for her words of wisdom. In life we're going to have to fight though some storms. Sometimes those storms may appear too strong. God will sent his people along to help walk through them. Some situations we may not be able to fight alone. We will need those people who strong to come along with us. I thank God for those people who helped me during my storm. Soon my storm was going to be over. About a month, my vision was coming back. We must be grateful for all the little things. Our health is very valuable. If I had to choose between my health or money what would it be? That's such an easy answer, my health. What point to have riches and be sick. Severe health issues, you will not be able to enjoy the money. Don't get me wrong. Having money is a need to get through this life. I always tell my heavenly father give me your strength. Where I'm able to work and make the money. We must thank him for our eyes, ears, hands, legs every organ in our body. The time I was at home. I begin to look at life different. What can I change about myself to be a better person. Changing me and forgiving will heal me. Forgiving I seen the best results of healing.

My last follow up with the doctor was to see how my process was. My family was so excited to come along with me. That day of my appointment. I didn't know what came over me but my attitude had changed. I just wanted to go to doctor along. Good news was about to approach my family ears. The enemy didn't want them to see or hear the power of God. The doctor came into the exam room. "Hi, "Mrs. Carter, "How are you doing?" I'm fine, I responded. His response was, 'Well you're great." Then he gave me the results of the recent test, that was taken. He had two pictures of my brain. The first picture was the image of the old brain. The second picture was the image of the new brain. The current MRI, the current test results shows no signs of MS. The second image of the brain had no tumors. The doctor was very impressed of how my brain was clear of tumors. His last response was, "Mrs. Carter you're fine." "Mrs. Carter continue to keep the faith. That's exactly why the enemy didn't want my family with me. The power of God was proven. I thank God so much for healing me. I thank him so much for waking me and my family. I thank him for our health. Each day someone find out they have a sickness. A sickness that can't be cure. Some would keep the faith and be strong. Some just have no hope. We must keep the faith and have hope. Never give up on yourself. We must plant seed in our lives. Plant seeds by doing good unto others. Helping others who can't do for themselves. I believed, I planted seeds for my healing. I worked as a caregiver for about a year. Some of the elderly, didn't like for anyone to care for them. I remembered this one lady. She always was upset. When you'll go around her. She always would be so mean. I remembered telling her to smile. She told me shut up ugly. I continue to show her love. I told her," I loved her." She said, You don't know me. How can you love me? I love you because I'm here to care for you. The more and more time in spent with that lady. She learned that I truly loved her. I thank God for giving me the heart is have. I thank God for the strength to take care of others. In life we should treat others as we want to be treated. One day I look forward to getting old. I never know who I may need to care for me. I make sure I respect my elders. I make sure I teaches my girls that same. We must remember we all are not promise to this world. We all are here for a purpose. We must find our purpose and accomplish it. Life is short. I want to make my heavenly father happy by doing great thing in my life. Why should I waist my life. I want him to know I appreciate him, by sending his only son Jesus to die for me and others. I tell my girls all the time," Never give up! Never stop, keep on moving in life. Show your heavenly father you appreciate your health. You appreciate all he have done for you. No matter what comes your way. Please keep the faith. I read up on Multiple Sclerosis. Once you're diagnoses with the diseases. Nine times out of ten, you're stuck with the disease. Most likely you'll have recurrence symptoms. Today for me I have no signs of MS. I move wonderful. I stay active. I enjoy working in my yard. I spent plenty times with my daughters. To my girls, I'm supermom. They say, mom you're supermom because you know how to get the job done. Today I'm a full time worker. I work as a paraoptometric. A paraoptometric works under the practice of a optometrist or ophthalmology. Job duties also provides the highest vision care to patients. This job I thank my heavenly father for. Going back to the problems I had with my eyes. The damage of the optic nerve. God place me in an environment, where I'm able to care for patients who have the same problems. I'm able to learn more information about the eye. It's so amazing how God heal me. Thank you father for your wisdom and knowledge. Thanks for your understanding to fulfill my job duties.

Seimeaka Quote

What God have for me is for me. Never let no problem or situations stop you from going to that place, God want you to go. Forgiveness is for you, not for others. Forgive for yourself !!!!!

9

What God have for Me...

I'm so obliged for God. No matter what may have came my way. He'll always find a way to change everything around. No matter how much negative came my way. He always brought out the positive. I always knew God had more for me. What he have for me, is for me. I'm willing to run towards what's mines. I finished college. I received my diploma with honors. I have a job in my profession. Finishing it all, I hade to keep God first. I remember someone telling me, I was asking for too much. I asked God to bless me with a job that fits the needs of my family. A job where I'm there for God. A job where I'm there for my girls and husband. A job where I would be able to grow with the company. Now how is that too much to ask for? The job I'm currently at, I'm the only black. I remember someone telling me. The place you're going they'll never hire blacks. My response to that person was, "What God have for me is for me." The same day I spoke that to that person. The doctor from the office called me. He welcome me abroad. I today, I'm still there. There have been times I felt like giving up. Then I realized that God would never sent you somewhere to fail you. I may be the only black. I'm treated fair as the others. I thank God for a change. I thank him for all his knowledge on the job. I look back over all I been through with my health. All I have asked him for. He blessed me with what I asked for. This job is not where I stop. There's more I like to accomplish. There's so much God showing me he have for me. I must continue to follow him and go get it. God giving me visions. I must achieve them. I must continue to seek more in my life. I tell my girls all the time never give up. Keep pushing for the best. Prove to God you're grateful for your life. Show him you're going to make the best out of your life. Sometimes the enemy will try to distract you. When he comes begin gloating about the goodness of goodness of God. I realized God prepare us for everything that comes in our life. I thank him all the time for preparation. Like a teacher prepare her students for an upcoming test. God prepares us for upcoming situations. We must continue our relationship with God, no matter what comes our way. We must find time to read his word. There should always be times, when we just tell him we love him. God is meant to be praise. God is to be thanks all the time. Thanking him and showing him gratitude of everything. God will begin to open doors for you. When God open doors for you, begin to go forward with no distractions. God have so many blessings for us. We must stay focus. Don't let anything or anyone side track you. Getting side track will cause your blessing to be push farther and farther. Example. You get ready to swing the door open. Soon as someone or something negative come in your view, you stop. Then the door close. When God have something for you it's for you. You must stay focus and walk into your door! I once read in the good book. John10:9 I am the door by me if any man enter in, he shall be saved and shall go in and out, and find pasture. One thing our heavenly father dislike is when we forget about him. He loves when we put our hope into him. He loves when we depends on him. Using him only when you feel like it, will get you back to the same situation. God is not a doormat. Where you only use him to wipe you feet. Having him all the times. You will find your situations easy to get out of. You will have the knowledge and wisdom to handle life situations. What comes in and out your life. A relationship with him. He will keep you in perfect peace. I can tell you everyday of your life is worth living for him. I realized the closer to my blessing. I had to change my surrounding. Some people will not rejoice with you. Some will pretend they're for you but not. God will prepare you. He will show you those people who's happy and whom not. It will hurt once you find out those people. It will be ok, once you realized those people was only hindering your blessing. Also the closer you get to what God have for you. You must continue to stay humble. Not staying humble when you should can stop your blessings. Our tongue is a powerful weapon. The tongue can destroy people with wrongful words. The tongue can cause a lot of trouble. It's up to you to know when to hold your tongue. Everything in your life depends on you. We have to be willing to make changes in our lives. To make changes in our life. We must be willing to pull up some old roots. We must get rid of old roots. Begin to examine every aspect of your life. Some want that change but they're stuck. The roots of believing you can't do this or that. The roots of old history that should have been left your life. Some bring up they hurt and find themselves stuck. We must put our lives in order. Being to write down, what you want for your life. Begin to write down all the hurt that took place in your life. Take that paper and throw away. You throwing away what's not good for you. Start with a fresh sheet of paper. Begins to claim new things in your life. Begin to put you life in order. Remember what God have for you is for you.

SEIMEAKA QUOTE

What God have for you, is for you. Never let no one block you, from what he have for you.

Jeremiah 29:11

For I know the plans I have for you, declares the Lord. Plans for welfare, and not for evil, to give you a future and hope,,,

10 | Release the Past, Better Future

Writing this last chapter, brought tears to my eyes. There was times, I thought I would of never complete writing my story. Times I felt like giving up. In my mind so many negative thoughts tired to stop me. Deep down inside I know I can accomplish anything with my heavenly father. I'm so grateful for the wisdom and knowledge my grandfather passed on to me. I'm also grateful for a mother, who brought us to church on Sundays. So grateful for all she was able to do. No matter what, the past must stay in the past. Her making sure we attend church was such a blessing. As a young girl attending church. I took in the word of God. As I got older those words, help me. Most of all we must take in the word of God and apply to our everyday lives. We must have a relationship with our heavenly father. I thought about this how can we have an relationship with him in heaven. If we don't have one with him on earth. Our father loves to bond with us. Having a relationship with God means a lot. We should always admit to him our wrongs. Building a relationship with God I had to learn to admit, what was wrong with me. He already know what's wrong. He just like to hear it from us. I needed to admit to myself, that I needed to change a whole lot within myself. In life our past experience can cost us to accomplish a lot within ourselves. I found myself walking around with scars. I had no choice but to get help. I attend counseling. Then I realized my father in heaven is more than a counselor. With his help in can overcome anything. My childhood,, seeing abuse in the household cause me to distance myself from others. I admitted into have trouble expressing my emotions. Seeing abuse as a young child cause so much trauma in my life. Some walk around this world holding in so much inside. We must release everything out. So we can live a better healthy life. Our heavenly father is capable of any and everything. He willing to renew us. We must admit to him what you see about yourself. Whatever it is within yourself that needs to be deliver from you. Trust in him and what the change. The more and more importantly admitted to him. He change every situation and made it better. I'm able to be happy and enjoy life knowing I'm not carrying around old baggage. We must start a new pattern. Don't allow your family to hear hurt. Repeating a bad pattern, can cost hurt to others. Hurt people, hurt people. We must not allow past hurt, to keep us hurt. In this world, I see so many get hurt, by close family and friends. Then you question, why they hurted that person the way they did. It's goes back to their past hurt. They been hurt and they hurt others. It's like they was raise to hurt one another. Like they was taught, it's ok. Instead of changing, some goes on and on. If there's anything that need to be released, please release it! Stop the pattern. Start your pattern in a different directions. Be willing to claim good over your life. Don't do what mom and dad did. Change, live your life different. I once heard someone say," Oh my mom did things this way. "Oh my dad did things this way. Well guess what, you're not your mom or dad. God created each and everyone different. Tell God you want to be like him. Tell him to teach you how to do things differently. He knows we're not perfect. When you're willing to do things differently. He willing to make things differently. Once again we must be willing to release what's hindering us to moving on. I realize some people are walking around with so much inside of them, that need to be pour out of them. Example, Someone eats a plate of bad food and that food so bad your stomach can't take it. Where the food must come out. Once the food have been released from the body, the stomach feels better. Anything that's not good for you. Release it and you shall feel better. Goes back to the example, life situations that came across your life. Bad situations, bad hurt, vomit it up. In order to walk right, feel better, we must pour all out of us. We must not let it stay in our bellies. Release it and leave it with the father. Get ready for a relationship that will never break apart. He'll never leave you or forsake you. I know my relationship with him is real. I truly love people. There's the ones I have to love from a distance. There's also the ones, I love that God say," Time shall heal." One thing about the heavenly father. He will correct you on your wrongs. Don't think since you build a relationship with God, that you off easy. I realized some do. We can't judge others because we feel that we doing just about everything right. Well guess what. Wrong again! We will continue to mess up. We should teach others how to accomplish a relationship with the heavenly father. He's willing to share his love with everyone. Never let man come between you and your heavenly father. Man will forsake you but God will never will.

SEIMEAKA FINAL QUOTE

I been on my own since sixteen. I have been forsaken by man plenty times. I wasn't afraid and didn't get discouraged because I knew it was him that stand before me..

My heavenly father have never forsaken me!!

To: My Earthly Parents

I love your guys dearly. I thank God for you guys. He needed the two of you, in order to produce me. When I felt like I was forsaken by you guys. I founded all the love I needed in my heavenly father. I couldn't allow my past hurt to stop me. For my father in heaven have remove that from me. The time I stay and stayed away was time of healing. We must not allow our past to stop our future. I seen a pattern that went on and on. I promise myself, I would stitch my threads in a different direction. To both parents if there any past hurt that have been buried inside. Please release it. Don't allow your past to keep you from building healthy relationships with your children and grandchildren. Showing you love someone's is not a gift or money. Showing you care is picking up the phone and saying ,"Hello, How are you doing?" Telling one another you love them. Time is not forever and don't get caught up with the things of this world. Now I'm a parent, As a parent we does fall short at times. There have been times I have to go and correct myself. I may have said something wrong to my girls. One thing I do, is fix it right then and there. I make sure I tell them, I'm sorry if I done something wrong. I learned from my heavenly father how to be a parent. I make sure I tell my girls I love them everyday. I show them I care. My husband make sure of that also. I never heard I love you from the both of you. Regardless of the relationship with the two of you. I must and will always love you!

CPSIA information can be obtained
at www.ICGtesting.com
Printed in the USA
BVHW080713010720
582657BV00003B/732